MissSettl

Kamden Ishmael Hilliard

Nightboat Books
New York

ISBN: 978-1-64362-140-1

Design and typesetting by Rissa Hochberger
Typeset in Janon Text and Protokoll

Cataloging-in-publication data is available from
the Library of Congress

Nightboat Books
New York
www.nightboat.org

*"i shall refuse to go to the moon,
unless I'm inoculated, against
the dangers of indiscriminate love."*

"Heavy Water Blues,"
—Bob Kaufman

M. Twain & I don't confuse learning w education or
autonomy w action / but these inspirational posters
see a nigga question our words 4 *SURPRISE !* The

goal of all knowledge is resistance ? Bet, lol , w / any
of these possible worlds out t/here ? Aristotle / was v
wrong / so luk a mofucca in the eye / try / take

insouciance 4 scraps & just liddat resistance comes
thru w the j / bops out the beer run quik / asks ,
in the ensuing gun fire , eff yr having ny fun? 1 time

boi of the club month liked " jailhouse drugs " / said
they make time smaller / Jail is a site of social
& bodily violence // feat. Capitalism / & if it
masquerades / as a place to / *TH INKA BOUT*

YR A CT ION S
(which it does)
than perhaps the microchimerical shrinkage of time

is / in factorial / a minor resistance / if not a 3rd tier
miracle / & if there's little freedom under G-d's seedy
thumb / why take shelter when there's rain ? It's fun !

I didn't organize revolution machines !
I didn't caste light w/out thota the mean !

Instead of *help* I said *save me , save me*
& sure sure I was good @that part ;
parboiled every pussing oodle of pressure .

Ya - , - Citizen - will - have - nd - Ya - , - Citizen -
dun - did - nd - Ya - Citizen - willing - 2 - do ! - nd -
Citizen like I meen like
"aw yu ,   boo fuccen hoo !" Yu , ain't never happen

2oo hard , now did yu ?
Now did yu   do this to me , too ?

Tried individuate deth nd these yts were really like
"you can have anything you want"

[i mean i did
kno] Literally
juss a bitch try
-na hav sum fun
herebouts , meatless
of the slice song . It go
slice , slice , slice ; quiet ; slice ,
slice , slice , quiet . No1ne kno
the length quiet go but *get this*
i've been here long enuff to kill
the orchid , mourn the orchid , con
-sider the orchid , love the orchid, try
life again , at 1nce , with the orchid , again,
also permanently changed by living , so
long , left so close to death . But I did
it ! Dressed 4or sex with the village
idiot if it keeps the drag on from
the children , so like lil biscuits .
Beyoung feelin' , I did not call
out *love* ; did not bit a tong
-(l)ue so hard it's out but
out it & still sumhow
tied up innit ? Iddinit .

4

Then , everyone dances

the Atmosphere

Dance . It goes ;

Gather , consume

& twist ! Again !

Some ppl

point [like ,

look ma , no

hand amine

take root

of it] , but

lol , yikes .

A spin of modern panic sets the day's strain .
The sadass stone . Squalor guild .
Str8 stoic as my A-line FISA warrant who
Cannot confirm my need 2 dent up a few neural certainties ,,,

                              BUT EFF IT DID , it wouldn't share .
The day is a " total top ."
After , it showers me in Wellbutrin
praise   Haldol praise
                        Amphetamine Salt daze .

& how now do my brain hurt ,
ideally , 4 1 attorney not 2 need a case in me .

Like : *What kinna wo rd is dongl e ?*
Why d o y u n e e   dm y I D ?
W h e r e h a v t h e y h i d d e n thewires ?

Fucction 4ward even *eff* movement is a matter
of concession 2 treatment , completeness , neatness .

Lure discretion advised , was advised , continued
to be advised—is like this : I wanted & I got gotted
anything to help me die : hot dog water   Panko facts.

Come onnnnnn

-nnnnn , Happy .

How bout song ?

Preservative joy ?

Happy , r frens

r tabled . They

expectint . So how

bout yu cure this

public uv me ? It's

half price , my teat .

TELLMEITISN'TACOGAY!HALFVICE.

ITCOMEFROMTHEVINETIME?OH,ITTA

BLEFRIENDSTIME!FRIEDSHIPSOFWHOL

TOWERFOODFRIENDS!STILLLIFEWITH

FRIENDSINOIL&GREATTHYME!WELO

E THESAMENESSOFFRIENDS,WHICHA

WAYSSEEMSTOFINDTHEMBEING"SOS

UPID,"AND,AFTERALLTHERACIA

ZEDCOLLEGIALITY,HAVINHAD"NOID

",BUT,WONDERING,STILL,HOWTOLIST

NIFYOU'RESOANGRY!ANDTHAT,YOU

KNOW,BEINGASITMAY,DOKNOWTHA

NOONEMEANTTOAPOLOGIZE

8

YOURFEELINGSAREHURT.KAY,PUMPKIN

Wow , Happy ,

this gr8888888

but how yu

r yu ta b   here ?

By my calculations ,

ya gotta feel

like gear play

preppin surge .

Sis , yu r here

inasmuchthat

I am here

& I am here

inasmuchthat

I don't want

to be you .

Don't clut among what matters the many gone dead

material gathering . Example :

It's 10 p . m . , do you know why

yr holographic blk people mite be

-yond smiling ? I don't dare the memory . You

have not seen this child . You have not .

The Wayans are actual bros. , so there's a hope . You like apples ,
crisis hot language quandary ? How 'bout them apples , titillated
with greasesheendinerboothbaddate cause i'm all *nah Tyler Perry
is whack af* . Cause when he ses it's *fun*
-ny tho   he AKAs *black people are funny*   which AKAs *blackness
is funny* which AKAs (O.E.D. here) : *Causing laughter or amusement ;
humorous* . Alas , crisis hot language quandary . Point taken . AKA
means *also known as* as well as *Alpha Kappa Alpha* . I keep asking ,
like Matt Damon in *Good Will Hunting* , if anyone likes these apples
but my apples are not Minnie Driver's phone number , they aren't
even apples ! The apple is never an apple , ask Eve , bruh . Ask Jeeves
clearly or you'll regret it . Fuck it , forget it : I don't think T.P.
is funny but i do think he's *funny* funny like (again , OED) : *Unusual
or odd ; curious* . Clotted sign , cloying signifier ; congealed New Rochelle
white sauce waxy over , yu guessed it , white noodles feat. steamed
Normandy vegetables . which means :

    A] strange , the stranger , & the strangest . a billfold
    uv snow . my mother dead yesterday , mayb 400 years ago .

    B] who doesn't want to eat but doesn't not want to eat or be awake
    or alive or dead or attached to these legs again ? Hu can show a little
    and live through the exposure ? Who can throw me up / ankleside
    / to the purpling sky ? Who can give me something 2o cry bout ?

    Better : who can give me a good reason why ?

it's ironic , yeee ?
the *Hawaiian way* 2 say , i mean . which mean /
steeltoe .   which mean / sugarcane .
i'm not , exactly , arguing that white people lack a certain ,
how shall we say… rhythm or respect but like… they do .
The writer of " Mele Kalikimaka " *&* i attended
the same settler preparatory proving ground , whose school
song limps 2 the tune of *O Christmas Tree* , *O Christmas Tree* .

1way would b

    think of the children !

another way say

    have ya thot of their children ?
& yet another may say
    yu can't sit with us .

Punahou School was , in part , a place
2 put missionary babies , & , in part , pocked
with the well-past aggressive aggression
gone passive in the plasticity o' paradise
lost in the neoliberal *get it get it get it got !*

a zillion steeltoes & sugarcane later ,
ain't nothing lyk Christianity in Hawaiian
(en the American South , en the footbridge
o' my mouth) 2 catch the heartstring
by the horsecollar .

the sounds each mean something
we need . i say
sugar cause i'm trying 2 b sweet
abt this, but also 'cause it's white (often)] .

& no , Punahou School alum

Robert Alexander Anderson isn't wrong .

Here we do kno *that Christmas*
will b green & bright   the sun
to shine by day   & all the stars   at nite .

Then the men hu arrive on a shore   & dispatch words
4 *mine*
4 *yrs*
 4 *isn't this fun ?*
don't yu love   this song ?

after Advance of Kansas Volunteers at Caloocan (1899)

Fresh out of   Filipinos ,   Edison and his crew
"" paid "" for African Americans , which is why they march

lack luster   says white film teacher . *Can anyone* white
film teacher asks   *tell me what might be revolutionary ?*

i like   how the rebels seem to be firing into the audience
like we are also in war . white film teacher agrees .

expounds . opens again   *any other thoughts ?* she asks .
the frame aligns us with the American fighters . how ? white film

teacher asks .
how ?

rebels stuff
their guns
step and fire   smoke fills the screen

rebels stuff
their guns
step and fire   smoke smoke smoke

rebels stuff
their guns
smoke smoke   smoke smoke smoke

rebels stuff
their smoke
and fall back   like smoke sweating itself out

rebels stuff   ed
with smoke
by the good ol boys

rebels stuff
the good ol boy waving a flag
with smoke   he downs like smoke stroked with sun

rebels stuff
themselves back toward the trees
back toward the trees   with blood heavy smoke

rebels stuff
is fucked up
the good ol boys have a new waving the flag   new smoke

rebels stuff   ed
into the edge of frame
poisoned pin pricks   no smoke nothing left to burn .

Reflection: Last lecture we screened *Advance of Kansas Volunteers at Caloocan* (Edison, 1899). Please compose some thoughts on the techniques, visual elements, and symbolism at work (open-ended , two50-500 words) .

2wo small details :

(a) Sergeant Squires   is v super important
flagella   uv our shiny nationalism
but the negroes for hire   have one too !
national gooey feeling   even a flag waver !

(b) after the Americans shipwreck up on the screen
and take their first shot
the rebels vanish
we may attribute this shit
2o a forgetful Edison ,
smoke's wrong hole .

who doesn't love a good war ? well perhaps
those getting shot . but then-- who doesn't
love a good warflik ? an opportunity tew get
choked out then choked up . eyes water .
eyes always water . Nickelodeons , some of
the first American theaters , could not show
certain films   for fear of riot. & aint tht luv?

                    hold me back homie hold me
back 'fore i dust this fucker . he don't even
know he aint even know .

Kansas did get p bloody . Kansas did get
p free . hot&preggers with grain . agro
-giant . Kansas volunteers as tribute .
& NO scream the mothers . NO kill sum1ne
else's baby they think . America war machine
go *these Filipinos wanta revolution, hm ?*
during the Phil-American war more civilians
died than soldiers . oops . troop morale
is caustic and bored . Genocide i believe
is a word . well so is winner-winner-chicken
-dinner-history-book-maker . not a word
but you feel me . the film reels is reeling me .

Goose Theory

The nēnē bird , AKA, the Hawaiian goose , AKA, how birds state need amidst emergency , economic development , pimped rainbows , & pricey neighbors : moar mayo , more honey , more hoodrich tricks dolloped w money$; modernization AKA mechanization AKA another system up--date blinging the bamboo man's bay AKA Kāne'ohe .

                                        & @10yearsold
                                     & @recentsettler

I didn't know what to call *duck* , *duck*, *goose* here (Oah'u, Hawai'i) / didn't believe cardboard could recycle . The *modern condition* guest starring as a *tradition of violence* . Race / Nation / Island -ism werked tis braintrain's

kazoo-quack .
            The thing about progress is a thing ; like Matson Shipping got the only birds on which the settlers agreed AKA bae-g-d AKA teh best excuse for speed . Neolib island living hard 4 sea bird need / glorious bellyfuls of toilet paper , peanut butter , tire tubes , & lube .

Dude ! , in what Nikki called , *the islands of Waikikiiiiiiiiii* , it's not the middle class that truckstick increasing bleed . No1 wants that fantasy novel . No1 plays my game ; goes duck duck Caught tryna swallo finishline shine around the noose knot . Cook the gold ; grind geese 2 the elbow grease ; the thing of things . How the word *kill* is taut only in an explainer on the word *survive* .

The Tetsuo Harano Tunnels Are Colonial Infrastructure !

This road takes me home , this road is a bypass , & this road
is under construction . Thus , the lane ahead closes ; narrows
in 1 mouth & out the other .

The US military made it thru the mountain w blasting
bellies full of fluff piece & infrastructure
bc the US Military put their objects where your objects is .
bc the US Military say " good night " .
bc the US Military say wine is coffee-life
& in-between the heart is a lonely house hunter ,
where we settled on freezing all the head(s) .
Something about stock , but I've grown
sick eating
    eating
    eating   the dead .

Down a golden hull : FAM ,   THE ! Alive !
& unguarded by the lite , the back gate ,
the mirrored finishes in Dadmom's bank
In Momdad's accounta the commissary :

capsa yt folx 2 rain & / peak down aisles & pocketluks
among wind / advisories

                  Pyramid Rock / the open water
                 / crook in2 me / outta me / on 2
my body . But , 2o swim is to say , *catch me if you can* ,
ocean . and who doesn't love   a challenge ? Who
after all these years   remains undefeated ?

What a trill ! : tidal boards all up in my beach
date like *oh y'all weren't finna sunset / buttfuck / cuddle* , *right ?*

Wrong , ocean .
rong , rock .
rrong ,
ugly little citizen-speaker . Ugly little U.S.
Gov't who , ofc , " reserved " 322 acres of Kāneohe Bay
for a military initiation : barbwire ID checks hoorahs
at the door like some dickly genuflect .

& the same ugly little
government-military who , in 1941 , " removed ,"
the upper half of " Pyramid Rock " downhill
from a gilded shotgun we occupied briefly

to make space for *The Minor Light of Oahu* ,
a lighthouse which guides
& overlooks government re/creation below .

But whatever . Some good shit ? Tides .
Change , I guess I mean .

Everyone loves you , they really
really love you , but there's that tide again :
dude shuffled yr lil music machine
& wants to know why yr bumping
                              what yr bumping .

(Who dons the crowd of dead adornments ?)

Anyway , the good shit is that in the 2000's
my siblings and I caught a Sea Cucumber
I , personally , named Hector & it was not
to dinner with we blind we mice small &
mad at , They wanted us to know that we
would *not be eating till y'all take care a that*
shit what did yu think was gonna happen ?

We thought the dream (mistake) of humane
(mistake) captivity (unnamable) . We
tried , lord , the plastic shovel (yellow)
as a stirrer , extra water for the bucket
(tho not a bucket but a sandcastle form
approximatin bucket function) So now we must
pour / 1 out lyk old time settlers
winkin from where we / tried luv / 1ce again /
& now are left wishin we didn't / er @least could
/ bury poor Heck bak blu / but alas it's backyard
 concrete 4 his immanent ass and as such

Herein lies Hector , The Sea Cucumber / removed
from The US Government's Marine Corps'
Marine Corps Base Hawaii's Kaneohe Bay's
Pyramid Rock Coastal Shelf bc we could.
Sorry for killing you . For property .

Simpl fact : " Disaster " was   " an unfavorable   aspect
of a planet or star, " having to do most   with " star crossed "
love .

So when he *does* ask , , , , , , , , if Hawai'i is " just lava " yet
I almos let him , , , , , , , the older white man , go

                                                    ne recently
                                        blind , as warned :

                            " UNDER
                        CONSTRUCTION ."

He scream *Take me ! Home ! Take ! Me ! Home !*

& *There* ,   I think , *now that's more like* lava : how backpay's payback dispells "
property ,"   re-settles violence ,

& animates the substance blind   teamsters of loss—

all of whom remind me   to drumbeat bacc   24 hr CNN
lava " disaster " crack ;

how it is for property ,   I wish Pēle's molt weed whack .

The bomb is gonna drop . So how will we kno
wat 2 call ' anxiety '   wen   we unbody ; un
man the mirror'd sky's tolerance of our micro
climatic doom ? Issa sustained lackadaisical threat :

death [& even inside , upon unravelling about the island , the subject still
carries   its qualities Threat] So lyk totally
pardon any thing i've done that don't seem 2 ask what
2 the slave is trade but expansion ? Pain ? The well
tailored industries of Paradise
                          Airborne [en per diem !] 2 flower
                          our own[ed] bays
                          our own[ed] sports
                          our own parts of entry

Wenever they drop the bomb   we'll b red
orange yello green blu indigo vio
                              lent / 4 the body moves
                          among destruction
                          & of the body's subsets there are
                          sum who'll will others gone
                Will want 4 nothing
                      but pentultimance : the buffer the buff
          'd stones of subjugation & product
Paper chase unburdened by others

Even en wastoidism : don't seem
like i'm giving up the free market
but i'm cumming, lol, just gotta
lessen my liquor . Find me big
green making button for my nigger
                          nigger nigger

Eff bastion of sadness
Then clots of threat

eff threat of sadness
Eff yu do hard dark

& thro the self from
lite then sort the body

by permissive distaste
Yu should stop but

like keep going it's hot
but i'm hurtfulhurting

Please , all my mes
Cum home

Omg yes shantay
yu stay fracka

A place of slave labor is not a slave place Ess a place of slave labor
People are slaves in a place of slave labor But b4 i'm just like here crying
again What lies amid the infanta of the slave is a question of travel : like going
Having a home Making a home How you know you aren't Are you a home
? May i b , 2 , Legal Guardian Land ? And then like transit social mobility
or the wet dream of nobility The slave identity is extant 4 those carriers of a
trauma so large G-d was like   *this cannot pozsibly fit in my car*

&

@TSA the (of course she is) woman has the *same last name* ! Lol
& i can't even offer shame Wonder even eff she kno my surname yt as the
freedom papes & market's grain or y i'm cocaine crop'd telescopic at 10am .

J & i joke about how we wash our wallets b4 air travel 4 neither 1
would court risk while walkin around in the skin they live us in .

Temporal changes in constructions of ytliberalism— & their yung-
er , smarter sibling ytneoliberalism & they cousin ytglobalism — demand
increasing systemic efficiency TL ; DR Smart phone users demand smart
violence & even be4 *that*

That , referring 2 the archipelago's 1st sugar plantations in the
early 1800's but really it's basic It updates & sends itself in2 the legislatively
slingy arms of the The 1890 McKinley Tariff Act .

An abridged list of resistances : work stoppage , abortion , wander-
ing from the field , opium , fire , work slowdowns , running away , extended
maternity , deviance

which was almost what i was meaning : my silent black & black film 4getting
thru TSA The whole flite full of fishy corn aerated red wine   The porcelain
pin My inward retch'd out

1 totally literal tool of power is mediated agency
The boi asks how i leave the island so often & i only kno what I've
willed myself against What I am unwilling 2 hav done 2 me any longer

The redeye must b lyk a blojob , gud aerodome .
Thinin in sumthin determined 2 b moved thru .
No1 maintain constant pleasure . Does air even
like pressure ? @the end of HNL : JFK a man
drove me 2 drink whatever i wanted He was what-
-ever I wanted , but didn't do pleasure . I thot
this was Buddhist , but dude asked on Mai Tais :
which rum would be best , he wundr'd , allowed ,
4 the road , on which he didn't want head . Mayb
I mean resignation is *no* for a nonce yt My frighty
fite thru the question of identity What it means
2 how a who yu don't kno or even hav done much 2 .

     1ce i flew & didn't let the men
do me in2 a *Yoohoo* . Drinkable . Clinkable . I stood .
Slept . I was quiet as I was kept . I saw a whole thing
about Bayard Rustin amongst bolts & stones
of onyx . I fell infinite & legible . I cried out
my leakages down the whole multitudinous avenues .
It's a living ! These clattered beads . Sweat .

I'm coolyea !
　　　Greatnow !

Know how it feels to harden
4 wat jump
the circuta pleasure , hehe .

It feels bad .

Got the note)*KICKWE*([funny
Administratively , but having suffered
medicine unsuccessfully , I come to-
-gether . Close .

Baffled by prix fixe harm . I am happy
as I am abandoned by song .

Had bread , salt , and wine .
Love's acute shelter amid ongoing loss .

Alternatively , G-d said to Job , " I'll tell you when you're older ."

So, here's to historical panic !

When I'll call on the energy of several white women ,
each waiting for their own managers , daring me do
demand the exact price sheets of forgiveness .

　　　　　　　　　I meen ,, issa big deal . Party ,
in the proper episteme , but not really here, where we've settled
for *pardon* ,　　　　　　　　　which begs ,

　　　　　　How, exactly,
　　　　　　　　have you been holding these 9/10ths?
　　　　　　How, exactly,
　　　　　　　　have you entertained discontent?

Shhhkmrp   in2o need's freeze , where i apologize
4 any gold standardsa goodness , which darn't like
    the party's going around to toast amid
   American red eyed mourning .

   There is a list of things to forget about
the beer , the nearbeer , the queer unfurling experience
of having had come a - top the Jumbotron's earILY
   loud arguments 4or sugar ,
   for the presence uv sugar ,   for what lies fallow
   of full food certification .

I'm exhausted by " light ." " Fun ," too .

The gub ' mint will not stop shutting
   up abt my problems & I still need to sober
   my problems ,   drive amid them ,
    & ice down the party   before it   goes limp
   in choppy morning waves .

Another round of funding . Another university . Another
Workshop . An Empire .

Another Whole Foods whispers
papaya papaya forever forever .

They gotcha *rainbo* / *papaya* / they (technically) gotcha
genetically modified papaya aka *GM papaya* / tho better
known as *GMO* papaya .

& what is " survival " but the transformation
of selves in the presence of possibility's impressment ?

I don't cum from here   or here   or here or   here , but i try
here 2o hurt each less & less each day .

Who is struck ? What grows ? How it do when modified ?
Where rots ? What brake the mouth ? Floods ?

                    I pass for a middling patron of beauty ,
                    but , sheit , the park does close in 15
                    so I guess giv'me here—

                    I'll swallow what you saveda me as long
                    as it's not not not knotted among a
                    portmanteau of power & the ongoing
                    institutional , systemic , and ecological
                    effects of its loss .

This paid programming is brought to you by the long handa
so strange plz killit w drugs
& i 2 would lyk 2 b killt w drugs ,
modified, made inoperable .

I elect a continued loose from reason ,
study it's freeze . Mourn dazzle .

Whassa Gaia finna do ? Mayb let/uce
starve ?- do ? Dip from this talk-a healing?

Just especial suspicion of *camoflauge* on pop-up shop runways—
the repeopled Pacific peopled by yt people's bamboo flooring It
clicks crass good , many toned , all , all crass good It clicks
perfect money into place insofarthat it is painfree :/ Pain free
Eco
    -logy . Mor like Ero
                  -tology lo ! 1 ! I swear on the sweating
    beat of sanity I mean sanitation I mean stratification
    I mean I'm a sure sinner , sick as a superfund But ,
    growing no moss   having been born to successful
    Black People of the nineties , so personal , so full
    of Property's bones and skulls and legally hooded
    garments and lynchings and immediate , unnecessarily
    explained violence Okay Ok Revision : There is no
    home , there is a somewhere bringing the bacon to .
    There is a waking up in the middle of the ride , some
    white person eating corn nuts , yelling , *i w ill turn*
    this w hole god ammn cent ury aroun d if yo u don't keep quiet !
                  & now ? After the dead man
                  's floatilla of it ?

            I grow concerned
            or like
            I am growing
            concern . Not like
            growing
            but like
            growin g, like *growing stuff*
                or *growing's tuff*

& eff you're trying hard not to hurt anyone
but yourself   & yourself is super shit   @ it
than i , 2 , have been beating back the green

with you , allalong , furrowed round joy's means .
I am so here ! So here to hav you here ! H!appy

how I am 2 tellya , about Happiness . Eff you
haven't yet heard of   happiness it's only bc

HE'S COM-ING 2 O GET YOU, HE'S' RITE BHIND YU

32

Things
do not
" get better "
they
" go on "
dancing

(it is my fear (of death (what will be willed in (passing? (Next (

nothing
careful
about
settling
the
moment

(Not until now (have I been (sold proof of (happiness & (honestly (I'm (

kissed by
bliss tho
suddenly ,
& unasked ,
I am
dislikedly
of it .

Our purpose , the peace , shall be absolute .
No secret conquest to upset this happy fact
of public , whose thoughts , whose purposes ,
are consistent with *made* life .   Nothing
peculiar to own peoples in interest of clearly
understanding .   Except , may be ,

for armaments of the population who secure
good will ; their distinguished healing made
all clearly recognizable peoples free
to determine the integrity of an unmolested
association of desire. Nothing to block
equality ,   whose creed runs all   Unless

the people of everything they possess put
their own   their own   their own

" grant ." Or how it all goes
down like *gotcha* shit .

No1 will take me upon
proposal : a cosmic ant-

-hology of shame ? " No ," 4
ample legions . How we

mite dievest of the tailpipe's
chug-a gluging . Or , hors

d'oeuvres divorced from
order , dioxin . Or how

the box I out
think does not exist ;

not unyielding nor un
yielding but rather is

an " opportunity zone ,"
" development program ,"

Proposal : nice sidewalks ,
very wide . Level . No concrete ,

maybe cork . Proposal : free
people forever . This

America *is* a solution as is
" round up ," a solution ,

as is orange —the agent—
orange —the color i love—

orange . What has been with
any application we might've

shared amicably ? I am ,
in parts , mourning color . I

am , in parcels , tryna pass
on gratuitous hope

RE MIND

May hang untended , grow toothy .

May satisfy force , win name .

May missletoe joy . May trip a life

& make out alive . May identified

mayhem misremember time's flinch

as an *oops* .

is greater than walking my woebegoneedness .
But not quite *the cow as yt as milk* , */ the cape*
as red as blood , */ the hair as yellow as corn* ,
the slippahz pure as gold . A put-on pragmatic

as musical theater . No sol'n , neither . Nothing
simple but syrup in the day's end . O but we
outside the box ! Wine . Knockturn alley sounds
like *nocturne* alley . Get it ? *So , you agree ? You*

think you're really pretty ?????? Well then , *you*
buy Momdad's Peter Pan , not JIF . *You* wait ,
windowless , in the clumsy cable hookup's
schedule . *You* soak sober till the sun's *end

scene* . *You* listen to Momdad movie quote—
or a bible movie quote Momdad [?]— *we do*
what we have to do , */ so we can do what we*
want to do — & always gotta be some bullshit

that want it's doing . Why else keep on yawning ?
The automatic teller machine machine , the 401K
stomping thru another strictly blasé day ? Until
Until Until— *surprise !* my stupid piñata face @

the dance @the gym from the flatfooted dactyls
of dayheadedness . It's me , the birthday toy ,
Bottoms Up ! , [made-up gay barre , reader (obvi)] ,
a case study in cringe , and sixty of our closest

co-conspirators . Having done what I must , I deed
doing to a tenable expression of love . Like ,
if money , then I mean my marks hard . Blood
gone good down the drain's gulp , which i know

like the sun opening another *scene* . This is not
fire it is
pure
sheen .

orRather

This yung-in' America killed for metaphysiqule ' assistance '

Knew patterned , endemic loneliness !
Was patterned , endemic loneliness !

" <u>Needed</u> " ' to ' ' fix ' ' **whatever** ' " went " **wrong**
" *Didn't* " **know** ' <u>if</u> ' anything ' " **was** " **wrong**

orRather

If An Apple A Day Kept The Doctor @ Play & I became what I ate ,
I threw up of what I feared .

Didn't wanna be an apple or see a doctor !

I was condemned into care   then
I tried   to make them apples   into lemons   then //
goofy   but not guaranteed failure //

orRather

The off / on of my body   flecked in freckled pearl light .
Sometimes he ,
got [me] *some , kid* .
Sometimes sounds off on my
medico-industrial chrysalis— as in
                    something to sign ,
                    as in to afford ,
                    as in *have it brought to the door* .

orRather

six to eight weeks of healing plaster
was too long, but healing *too long* ?
I kinna liked that .

orRather

DO YOU SEE ME STANDING HERE ?? TRYNA ? ?

Enlitened wytdudes couldn't never be content
2 luk @the sky [jus luk] or lack an explainatron .

i can't read myself from public niggardly precog-
-nition , tho I do kno epistolmythology is a

branch of philosophy dead
icated 2 the study of knoledge . Humans make shit ,

fine ,
but couldn't we make sumthin' cooler ?

Fucc this volcano proj . Frack dese anglo pickings apart .
Why i ain't gota a lick uv sleep

closer 2 the centera this here coochie pop / sign
& signal fire .

After all i've read , nothin' litens my load er lessins my head
nor explains the word 4 what has agreed 2 hold me .

Oh bother , oh brother . I ain't dead yet ! See ! Even me three !
I talk , waddle my walk thru poems , tip blanched black w heat .

Took order as destiny .   Had 'em *for here* ,
agreed that   *offcourse you had best   intentions* .

But in a blur of mean[. ing] , whip, & search
for America's Next Top [Solvent] , I head

said *yes* , *behavioral joy* ; tookaway lessens
from removal . Like , IDK , what *may* a nigga

say but she were told : *Learn !*   & did
fuck the alturnativ : that I *were* happy to see

yr phone if tht's not yr phone unpocketed , plumpin me .
& yet the hell about me became the hell

smelt withon me . T'was a watermark'd sum-
-mer ; lots of personal feelings . Unfuckable

as I fell in *only a ride* to the altern , thinking
motion worked liddat . & where ? Enthere ?

It is a party , but I want nothing to do with
light . Look at these teeth I am   glowering .

MONEY PROBLEM

With money 'm even more wonderfilled ! & wen holdin' w/ pattern , I buy food 4or

my Future Earnings Potentiality . Yet , given water , the herein described refuses

to rip into me & mine & my own & black homeownership but damn fuck shit this

whole time thought   there was like   an *award*   for money   but there is no

award . There is no money . There is no bad of mine to have had and in fact

I am not " BAD " w money   just drawn red 2 impent absence   gaped goal itching

each tik'd minute spent mintin pre-op o' the Apocalypse   & look I was proud , even

swallowing but now I'm like   *would never* .   *Lol* ,   *no thanks* .

Nigguh elves / small   kine as color +

   queer   Lol ,   lyk , *w0ah*   *Weerd*

      Dancers aspring & annals   o' my mammalian

   annuals   The longing day   my fairy eschew

empty calories ,   macho cheese

                              2 move in2 me a mischevious safety

b/w STONEWALL   & WPA2 WIFI

                        I got a passing

                        encryption ,   cruel

   as the sign's out from queerdum / 2 upheel naturality

stay sentience   2 suppervillancy & bigone it /

                     Who'd a thunk in thru pain 2 *pass*

abreast of the butcher& wrapping& rolling& paper

            bag ? Lest @last / call my luv is bhind

   the 8ball of mortar Nothing

but division   settle in2 such varial sinonym

      Exclusionarily hi

, major ! Solitude ! Say it so ,   quik   solo ! *We*

weeeeeee *are never ever ever / getting back 2githir*

eff the social imaginary got sum 2 say

No future No immigrants No *free*

      PDF amongst pastoral encryption

   1 wundr   of the world ,

               the kingdom , the ever

clottd dream of danger

   Uunaquainted trees & the displacd

problem   o' open access

                     2 legibility .

Y'all got warm socks on Earth ?
Gr8 ! So why dream terror , finally
having arrived , @ rest ? Oh , bc

you can't *win* if you don't *believe*
in change overtime ,   I guess !
However , Ahem , Ah   em ! This

situation actually , this   situation,
actually sensectionalizes my
my!sk-i!!s! L U C K E-LUCKE

me , ushering so luckily , so
welcome in The Preemptiv
Theater's trouble 4or your

seeing Every Peoples , all Registered
Users , & Affiliate Institutions .
We jusso *worried !* about me . We heard I

Resisted   the ideological hold & feared the sea
   Queried   the ideological hold & took *so long*
         Abdicated   the ideological hold & hav questions

Like , I'd like to know , like , how cum Country gets 2 b
a fly on the wall of his own rushing node ? Streaming 10-80-3
[rd]-personhood so real yu can't step innit 2wice / sheit yu can't step

   innit 1nce Yu can't   sheit-chu fit the skull tho , huh ?

      You coming intact tho , huh ? You 10-pig !
   You fingers ! You delicious paddles !
      You autodidact of the anthropocene !

You who fail to come clean ,
            who decants the millennial dunes ,
      who resists regime change . *Really* ?,
you pray , you , who say , *Yowza are things like   this bad ?*
& , lol , I have come only to tell ya that
      Yowza things are so much worse .

& cool , sure , yeeeea , I'm with it ,
like , idk   haven'tchu prayed
           on a plane till it   pivot ? ?

       Emplode-e of the Month ,,
       @YrEmptying ! Reporting bootie
                    4or where I wanted
                    the flag (I wanted the flag
                    where I was a coherent
                    sobject & sumhow—

                    Yeah , I guess ,
                    I did it !?

                    Didn't hav any trouble
                    for a time , trouble
                    believing innit . . .

         Yet Nahnah I k!d ! I Kid it ! Here I stan still

finna kill it from the limpest erattan   of orbit !!!

Like, IDK , life is embarrassing .

@ the end lie plastics ,

bad feelings , bad plastic feelings , a practiced *whatever tho* .

        I can explain this eff you like see me flail .
        I can contain this eff you'll watch me fail .

Past 11pm's postup , ramen , & menthols , he still commands
orbital agency . A jeep 12niteripe w fluorescent tumbleweeds

of packaging . All the cheap lite wonders
now SHOULD i COULD i WOULD i weddingring the bong eyed boi ?

Lazy fingers toy a sticky torso   'gainst torn pleather .
This boi has my eyes rubberized 2 manholes & this boi
has my eyes however he'd lyk 'em , 'cause yes , speakerself
falling in love with another straight boi is not their fault :: shitty ramen ,
thAt giggle , this nite warm as a cherry cherrying itself . . .

                  but thankfully i'm used 2 it [whatever they party favor
                  or makes me party to].
He howls into the bong , wildeyed , & swallows the cough [just the cough
                        (but a boigirl dreams,
                        teems sick with steam)].
suppression   is a talent   i would kill
                myself 4   but really , so is love
& so is being loved.
why else yu think i'm kickin' it ? the only explanation 4 this life & its continu-
ing lung capacity . so this is best . this will do & does

me , cloudy in jeep   blunted
              w wanting 4 the boi .

Uh , hi ,   Mx.-Race-'Merica   Yu hav an account
2 settle Start up that labor shop ! Don't shimmy !
Don't think less about yr self in the next want
unnozzled !   Even the ditches would sell
4 the rite   of unmolested assembly ! *Lookit this stuff*
isn't it neat ? I got an outbox in lieu of a body ,
tapas , pupus , & aperitifs 4 the same purposeful doing . . .

But yu thot 2 leave   unchecked . . . Luk ,
we all talk We all no yu owe dis plastoral nite
a wallet wingéd A wallet emptied A wallet
wide w knowing A wallet w doors & wind
ows A slim fit feeling lyk pig's blood
down the money clit & unfortunately , our payment
programs can't even w yr hard cash   We
don't self-identify as —lyk— super superior   but are
watchful sounds. Selfish mostly. We dlite   American
as an almanac of Afro-Diasporic aphrodisiacs.

These delicacies ain't a decision & disruption of such
articulates yr racial future in memorandum!
     & of yr alleged " nigger wealth, "
       it seems yu wish
2 pack it all back in2 a nameless thing.   Really nude
color'd 2 nothing in a honest presentism !   What eff
we banished the astral bit [the drool the info holder
tool] & really considered how being named is like
the end of possibility ? But O , Kam , yu kno , what 1
won't call themselves 4 what 1 will
scrub themselves nameless   Risk 4 thrill.

No tears No tips No meters No nips [well
Mayb] No Lyft No Uber No 1-8
hundo But he wanna kno *How yu been ?*
   Where'd yu go   & why ? [whudda guy won't in

-ter desire] So tho [y'all] *didn't start
the fire* He galk ya down Ugh a drink
-hir Satisfied ?   Now asks of MomDad &
   late nite desires   Till so close yu go

Southwest Delta American Air lines
Any   *Here*   *isgud*   *Fine* : the metallic ,
edging departures of queer luv-kin Shipped ?
   Sure , yu guess Yu need 2 move on But fucc !

What danger cost too much , Patron saintof
Patrón ? Skychaplin , dis politic ain't
got a pot dealer 2 piss in   Yu-Me ?
   Peppery as an amphetamine Pee

pull'd as a population restriction
Shirtless i'm serviced ; shoeless i'm nervous
I'm saying in everyway I've been
   seen @ all   the desks , submitted   Sordid

Like one fuccpiece etherized up ontta turntable , the gym-tan-Chinese
boy in the lingeriette got my eye / *boy? love?* / but I warn't murk any

gender mayb / there's my river / me heart's cherry top / spacey &
transgressive bc I luv boya the month club's frown flower'd , let it queer

up which ever tree . This time , *if you're a bird* , *I'm a taxidermist* . I kill speech
to dead contentions . I carry force grammatic : Ex : the *it's* of , *look* , *it's*

a figgernaggot require an apostrophe as it detonate *being of* not *possession
of* / self which , alternatively , is to get one's *location blown* . Lol . I know .

I'm pre diamond dark   honey   jumpcutting thru *limited time*
        offerings 4or free . 99 !
Less me ,!   with my shapes nd shit / fractured fractal :

gay bro girl toy / black mutt mix drink   stirred and shaky
tryna be decent with my grey goose / Gatorade ass All *flattire flambé*
so fuck if i'm spending 18 on a cocktail

cause it's in a mason jar   thrifty / flirty / shifty me
with my continued attempts at (in)visibility
soupy self jumpcutting nonetheless at Hula's with the willow

lily white boys
but truly friends , Romans , cunt-rycreeple
lend me your cauliflower ears for a final song request :

if it please the genital massas   i mean

misters out there   wash your doggone eyeballs

before ya go falutin em up my brotank ! ya silly

strong suited fellas !   i'm just a sow   please

take a shot of this milk   white as your gooooood lovin !

BOITROUBLE

Wet as he rolled in2 me I b / still
am / are / dappl'd in his *he*
[bak, booty, taint   glitter'd w gleam].

I do the day
2 day : cart my cream
fill'd chavity from   EXCHANGES&
RETURNS bak

      2 propriety / after a public water-closet-post-up-&-prop
with a pleasant stranger who art the apartmint

en me— but still ,
we spin on
stupid . Desire
a mark .

Again .

Heaven .

"The sun beats lightning on the waves,
The waves fold thunder on the sand"

—Hart Crane, "Voyages"

BAD DIRECTIONS

No need to brag about it , Mr. Crane .   We know ! You're smart & pretty . All love is terror ,   but still , isn't the sea beautiful ? Halfway thru happy hour , grinning tipsy

toward another horizon ?   Yes , riptide is dangerous , but isn't that why we have band aids & comrades ?   Shoulders and spry cordage to sink us home ? If i'm gonna

drown , i thot ,   the titanic isn't a bad thot , i thot , to take best model and torso . All conduct is love . All sand was once Heineken whole shell . Before it was all   *don't eat*

before you swim & now it's all *never binge on an empty stomach* . 2oo often I've been in the shorelegs of a boy I couldn't quite kill . The only thing to depend on is change :

today then tomorrow ; black blue yellow and reduced swelling . He may not have read Melville , but he is alive and wearing the fuck out of those highlighter pink boardshorts

& the way he's looking at the way i'm looking at him means this is fair : we paddle out above *fresh ruffles of surf* & drown the gorgeous way home .

hi , he says .
hi , i say .
how are you ? he says .
i'm good . and you ? i say .
good , he say , *i've been rereading harry potter* . he say .

which ends it, cause

1] i'm finna fuck, not recall my reading habits
and 2] the novels , all seven of them , have five , yes , five , black
people . i am five , yes, five black people . my complicated
fragments of code chimerical limp
3] the transphobia

but what do you do ?
cry ? cut yourself
out ? yes , but what else ?
roll out of bed and into another day still delicate
from dreaming ?
whisper,

> *please , baby ,   i know it's hard , but   try sleep .*

I'm science   sure ! Like , look , I , 2 , would lyk 2 b
startin w objects in the mirror ; closer than i cohere ;
queerer , 2 , clearly :

quasi-hypnotic hostility , a-doodle-do
from requeerin this body clock

> So werk bakwards
> Wonder down worry
> Get wordy

I hav 2 thank the academy 4 mi honor gap , thihole …

I just wanna say , *omg* , *ily*   2 !
Luv is a gr8 verb but what it do wen

i've packed this bowl 4 2wooooooo
& i'm gonna wanna   smoke it w
yuuuuuuuuu ? ???

lol but do [gotsta] kno   y
a nigguh kno this many
combos , or , most formatively , Disney's steel corkheel of retreat , or

RB + Y + TELEFONE VOICE + trigger down
> *trigger down*
> *!*

ong story short : statsprof couldn't figure his computer machine so he called it *schizophrenic* .

short story long : schizophrenia , which does , in important ways , pop from the Greek root 4 split , does not— 4 1nce & a motherfuccing all— hav nything 2 do w personality , but refers 2 a split betwixt personhood & external reality . the schizophrenic is not multiple ppl or necessarily drooling & on their way 2 kill yr children . & in fact , the schizophrenic is at greater risk of violence from others than the [ew] average folx ; & in fact , there's no *schizophrenia* but a spectrum . it's dumbasses lyk statsprof [ytqueer , summa the worst , i tell ya / complete w a flat-footed Midwest crack-cent] hu think medical conditions r adjectives 4 shitty tech .

but hu am i 2 critique sound ? oh , right , a person . a kinna person , also , hu havin been hurt by language , understands , intimately , powers of the gutcheck , of *that's not what i meant / of don't take it so seriously* .

tho , thankfully , this person down row from me raises their hand [not 2 b , i think , called on , but rather] 2 inform him // yr *computer does not hav schizophrenia & medical conditions r not code 4 poor performance , xoxo , gossip grrl*

anywayz , yt queer affronted & shit . lukin lyk a poorly attended dinner party , & eventually says   *i'm sry eff my language offended yu //*

sm-fuccin'-h .

SUGGESTED APOLOGY PROMPTS 4 WHT
QUEER OF THE WEEK THT JUST MAKE ME
MIGHT THROW HANDS RN :

sry that i said a fucced up thing or
sry the fucced up thing i said was hellastupid otherizing or
sry i actually believe in my own whiteness so fervently or
sry i've lent credence 2 pervasive narratives of mental
illness *not mental* ***health*** or
sry 4 my mad public ignorance or
sry abt the way i've used my institutional , physical , social
, & academic privileges 2 mobilize shittily held personal
beliefs abt the ways in which schizophrenias & academic
performance r mutually exclusive smh i'm an asshole :(

but nah , statsprof is sry abt our delicate feelins . lyk valid critique of social ableism is conditional , lyk it's a decision 2 b damaged by language , lyk we shouldn't *read in2 things* so much . it ain't a decision but what's new ? i'm just tryna trap thru the day wout crying wen statsprof's MacBook freezes / & the lecture freezes / fuccs up / fails / fractures / goes *schizo* .

worst was post-class , wen i got drawn in2 a cig-circle / where erryone was so surprised *she ?   idk what it is ? she probably ?   // you're supposed 2 call them they but whateverhahaha //   nyway i'm so surprised that she went all PC NAZI on him // right ?   i* offered *yeah, but he was kinda fuccy* . i offered a cig . we smoked it fast .

Effective domination is *self* composed ,   tonguing each whole note of sorrow .

Lotsa *hey hey stop bitting   yourself stop bitting yourself beb beb* . Thus , I've gone

catty , cunty , dragging my Black Upper Middle Class Ass through the country ,

composing an imposing positionality among alum sweaters . But then again ,

the university ought to die . But then again , something about the *quad* . Those

frisbee drugs , striping saliva up every joint , every which way day gone wrong

along want for preindustrial assistance . & 4or y'all , folx ? That's all , folx . IJS

— resist Love , 4or love is a trenchcoat money stack . & The University is late

2o lecture . Again . Chews they pencil , yesterday , now , always , again , which

is gross - hot , def yt people shit . The University didn't mean to offend that hair , but was just so demographically curious about where you come from . Give it

where you come from , always , again , yesterday , now . Get credit . Take it . All

-ternatively , DON'T GO TO COLLEGE . Like, will you be happy 2o be here , ya

talented tenth inch dick click / clit bait? I was not happy to be there , reader . I can

only

tell

you

I

was

not .

Dequantes Lamar reps Rich Homie Quan , & i , too , do not tolerate want ,

even for a nickname . my fav Hamlet [in *Hamlet* , obvi] is Ethan Hawke ,

not Mr . Branagh . there go my shot @hydromaticL0VE , or cokeing the boy

-of-the-month-club from his collared . alas , poor Yorick didn't trap in the late

evening's taillite , so i tick thru 2 the left scrim's cold plite . formerwhtboifriend

said *Dequantes is a nigger name , gets the need 4 a monicker* . I didn't evn add

the former that time talk abt a ginuwine commitment 2 sociocultural ascension

via association 2 ytness . now do i kno what race do , even 2 the dumbest skin .

not that i L0VE[ed] yt bois , i L0VE[ed] the bounties of ytness , the possibility

of palatable politic ... do i wanna b right or effective ? am i wrong 4 both ? dis

ashy Ash Catch'em ass has turnt in me a proclivity 4 decimalia . formerwhtboifriend
meant [b careful , they always meaning some shit] : Dequantes is a nigger .

the Homie Quan is nigger rich . hitch the husk under spotlite & sprout dollars ,
minty fresh morning breath , coffee , sugar , the killing crop , the crowded margins

of this shitty mystery novel [why call it history ?] . why wish yu was a little bit taller
/ wish yu was a baller ? or more stevia splenda sacrilege / or that yu couldn't sus import

by size . the way Americans love trade [AKA slaves lol] & social crapital . i shld lyk
Mr. Branagh more than i do , but i kno wht a monicker is / can do / shields frm / makes

into . 2 make out of / or off with / is dangerous . 1 self when yrself isn't treated super
much lyk a self it is the risk of 1 head 2 lop or 1 place 2 pop the bottleneck . as a living

thing , i was nvr sure : codeswitching ? coatswitching ? fractalized ? bring the contrast up ?

GROWING CONCERN

Nao , nao , don't *wannna* swish up Real American Tragedy
4 The Older , o my Brother ; watt doubled what a botherer ,
[don't *mean* it , leasewise [in the trenches of childhood
[I mean all malice in mere apocraphy tho ! So heartsniffle

burns well within my bailywick / a struggle / strapp'd w bodies
& B.O. & birth order & chip'd shoulders Hatred i want 2 mean
Dream hard as 3rd degree a la / steam // Upon this Time Only Once ,
bless me / lol // 4 as kids , Brother donned a sickness .

CALL NOW! 1-800-weaponized-biologics now ! & 4 a limited time

nahnahnah

THE OLDER's brand new sick —circle wink— A spot A spoon / full
of pain 2 make the medicine make the skin drain
It was ringworm ! The edge / of death! No , glory ! Nah , death !

/ Lol / social & only slite // he geffum   *woah*
weird   worm [itchy it does /] parasite / yet still /
so many friends ! Friends ! He has / so many friends / his friends
are carefula me & mine , too / are careful 2 b his primarily ,
memorialy , yet upon attempt of articulation of luv amidst change
& growing pains of the institution —sorry—yes— this is a story
about my older brother who once had ringworm and I remember
deep pleasure at seeing sucha perfect thing join me amid
the qualities of stigamological consciousness .

For this reason ,
I generally feel ess important 2 stage death / get close w a bitch
/ drinks in the good dark .

THE OLDER is disgusty [4 1ce / 2 b honest] still free from significant
trauma / so DUH , MOMDAD to the rescue MOMDAD vote , own
property , & pass care , suspiciously , in2 science 2 salve / sort /
safe 4 children— save // So no / THE OLDER don't die / drat /
" would have gotten away with it 2 , [ef]f it weren't for yu meddling
[sciences] !" Kidding ! So DUH / MOMDAD : caped thing 2 put a trap

in that mass / thick quell / stomp the curve's bite / *chomp* / *chomp*
chomp / & / The world is hir's 2 clingwrap

2 save //

But no lol no no don't depose my petty depositories Dunno even
wat i'd do eff a most filial desire darkened my stoopkid ,
let in the strange significance of lite / best case :

Climate change science , having received its final dayurnal deification ,
is unfucked with ever again . True racial capitalism fails . True capitalism
fails . Failure catalogues . The beautiful , unknown disaster occurs—
we persist— yt fortification dies . Yt supremacy dies . White People die .
Sylvia Wynter takes up a part-time gig running Zamboni at The Center
for Black Respite !

The Older lives ! / in glorious strapsa cell & muscle
The Older learns *I hope you die first* mean luv but my shit wish remainsa
itself frequently *I hope you die first* insofar that living without you feels
like a task i am unprepared to undertake // The Older lives ! He builds
a family with his wife (yes , he has some heterosexuality , as a treat)
and works and laughs the gigantic laugh of complete balance and joy
// I hope you die 1st I hope you die so i can mourn you with flowers
and laurels and art and sound , because i cannot bear , even the image
of you , alone of me , mourning me .

I guess , my essential concerns are of quality , uncomplicated , anti-capital
existence based in Pro-Black Life .

Sometimes these damages are delivered only to save ,
only to teach , only to demonstrate how love comes back in , always ,
to where it always was , bit by bit .

FINAL LOVE POEM

Not *green*   , but the thing the word sings , but your eyes ,
that microforest slitherin in my knowledge of love . No
social media catch my cliffjump outta this world fat green .

Banish my sad ivy (it's shit envy) . Emptying coke into
my empty . Opting to extend my perversely Lenty abolition
of care , of concern —I was CONFUSED— I was contused
by love , thus ends the excuse tract . Time's laugh track .

Like , luk outside , there are trees ! & they're all different !
With leaves & nettles & that's why I'm an agnostic , why
I resist addiction . I promise , Chase , I'm a dull bore fore
boxy light . Additionally , lol , you do not have green eyes ,
I know that , but consider your face (looking @my face) ,
Chase , how green , how new & more & growing , we feel .

SELFI . E .

Myne ! Me person ! My face ! My ball at the gym
Me flash foto only one hr finish off me shit on
meself / A-E-I-O-Y & sumtimes / ME million
murder feeling / MomDad / remove the ancient
mariner / 4 his 2XLooken down mi   sumtimes
silly lil' self / sometimes sopped up-lilself (secured
only 4 safety 4 harm's loud lettering (// Yu down w

MY
pp ?
Ye
yu
kno
I
mite b

   the figur
   disolft ,

    categorically nuclear ,

    SPLITFUSE in a forest   then no more forest

     Must i be sorry 4 my making flat meat ?
     Like , if there's no1 4 my grizzle   am i still a feast ?

Fell sorrow's small intestine ; order a cosmo witcha
real shoulders out from under chuffed collar . Want
finally fleed – walk – wake the military domesticc's
tight bounce, coin , backup . Still made ; easy lying
down innit (cause I made it .) Prefer this 1 , where
we burn down innit . I think about that statea me :
overwhere , deposed , squirrilish , squiggled , squeakin '

on to something else , no doubtedly , detestably .

America has no *regime* but social lawlicy . White terror
opens with plea— a guilty putterng : *Pardon , I'm saving*
this seat for a friend . Pardon, could you help me find out where
I'm coming from ? Pardon , I've taken the counterhegemonik turn
@ 25 & am stressed by the con of compliance . Pardon , just
got caught up eavesloppin who ever in this dive decided exactly

who I might be .

When i bopped about
hide-a-key coke copping in [this literally
happened] A crab shack bathroom ,
                                    A McDonald's bathroom , The Famous
House Party Bathroom
But i don't do crab   coke   or McDonald's nymore
or cataracts of sorrow   or the way sumtimes   without warning
wind would pull   from me
          my thousand hundred   pipings .

Unstopped not even   eff   i do luv
a lil' death in me .

I don't even want reparations

yet ! First , I will take a #3 combo
bc i'm hungry and a #2 pencil ,
not cause negros remain unprepared
for ontological warfare— but bc
I need to jot all this down ;
every vector of extra-legal , state-
sanctioned , conspiratorial ,
anti-accidental violence . See— look—

I all ready need another pencil
— in fact— gimmie a pen to restrict
all war criminals of Yt nationalisem :
they're Dicks , they're Cheneies ,
they're Fords , and Black Gold ,
their hawks , there geese down .

This is carceral feminism insofar that
when I conduct G-d's forgiving audit
of yt time (its punctuations ,) I am left
with the whole ass reality of global
terrorism and crimes against that there
humanity a yall's (whole nother poem) .

how with the metro/tube/transport machines ?   how with the laws ,
not quite opaque enough ?   how with the racisms ?   and of all
these aberrations   how is racist   for sure racist ?

definitely the eyes ! the eyes scritching my velcro folds
get me loud af .   feelin' pretty   kill the master and marry his wife .

the dead don't travel well and living makes these unravelling conditions
sound so swell .   someday   way back home is waiting flashbacked
and flushéd with rememory
                          and rolling up all at once   like ::

        ma and i are about the last minute shopping and it's about the dessert
        though it's not about the apple pie .   cause the apple pie is about
        baseball   which somehow makes my throat feel a bit noose-y .

Fside from our *LET'S WATCH*ing of *A DIS NEY
CHA NNEL MO VIE* / FAM , THE is the first
& most final of moral universes Always same Nvr
change! / Have A Kick Ass Summer!

As such , Luv's frequency 4 us [*we3 tweens of Orient—*] twas
/ *AY, MA* / or / *MOOOOOOOM* / but i can't
recall our Pops call Do kno the dialtone tho Do save him

Dead number defunct Whatever I might have wanted
would be disgussed later but in a sêance more lyk *CATDOG* ,
twas never metalk or selftalk but wetalk

bc who could want 2003's *Daredevil* / 8pm ?
You . You could want 2003's *Daredevil* / 8pm .
bc a boy wants you some way & definitely

wants 2003's Daredevil / 8pm / bc yu want a boy's shoulder
press stats , you want to learn them at nitetime & so / *AY, MA* /
goes gr8 but wants / nay / *needs* 2 discuss w Dad , wants me
2 request by text / & i can't think won't / think *damn* ,   *the number don't--*

so we go out ,   we get fucked   up , we get up an alleyway , and suddenly
it's gorgeous : three Scottish dudes , drinks [double vodka with soda   which
should not be a thing but is and oh are we thankful for the free drunk], and the
evening's colander spiked with light.

until he's not that cute 'cause now he's asking if my dick is a   *big organic black dick?*
until my drunk tongue snorts   *i'd rather be the kind of person that has yellow fever*
than the kind that answers you with want .

revision : totes made out with him and the two other imports [drastically improves
my batboy average].   don't tell Ma or my friends .   also   the co-workers
aren't always *that* racist (right ?)

AND SEE SEE YOU ALMOST BELIEVED ME !

with my facts and book learning !
Let a black grrl loose in a library
and you'll understand American slavery .

I'd be nervous too , White America , Fight
America under a god divisible . I studied ,
so I know *amaze* really means that's dope as fuck THOUGH I'm also scarred
I mean scared .

My doc used to say : *the best indicator of future behavior is past behavior*
and yalls asses still don't see why I'm nervous All The Time ?
why All The Time feels like it's ready to time me the fuck out ?

I am egg on my own face , and something smells real red white and blue
round here but mostly red , mostly something I'd read in the paper , read
as long as I'm not the dead headline and sinker .

*"an isotonic rehydration sport drink launched in Hong Kong in 2011....
specially formulated for those who enjoy a healthy and active lifestyle,
suitable for...hot weather or sweating occasions."*
   —Coca-Cola corp.

faster than a speeding bullet   my gullet poached with steam :
Aquarius !   here to ply my wet dream . nine hunnit and twenty
milliliters of hydraulic lubrication and Coca Cola product to rock
my western ass to sleep .   crampless , campless the woes
of my white whine and deedless hands .   Mrs. Bishop knows :
travel is a needy needy boy ,   but there's always you , Aquarius .
kissing on my ethnic booboos , my vegetarian barracuda ,
my constant reminder of capitalism .   like cigarette smoke
caught in cotton .   Hong Kong we poppin bottles   of Aquarius ,
ticking through the streets   we bombed out hilarious .   the point
is product   and ain't you one sharp ass star , aqua love ?
quick prick in the dry mouth of sky .   eleven pins popping
the tumbler under my tongue   all blue tasting , thank you thank you
thou art a minor-love god   all hydrating and completely recyclable .

trika treat / turnta feat
gim   / mie all dat gud /
heat   eff ya darn't
i don't   care i'll pull
down   me   underwears
                    & glo

deviance is a candy

coda i'd snap chimeric

/ limp / glottal w lite

/ but will [smh] let

a nigguh live //

i'm not hard 4 / or on / white

sugars / so what of

the state's legislative buttstuff , decried in Lawrence v. Texas ?
slootin down All Saint's eve / weavesa red
lite & hurt // 2 dress rehearse
my movements /   hearse-ward
the self runnit / lines / try its blockin 4
multi culturalism day , crossdress
day , drag day , black history
month , girl's day—   permitted
formz 4 resistance

here's a song

here's a reading

list / here's a treaty

here's an updated terms

and conditions agreement

here's a momentary redress of

grievance

I 1stly flirt bc my visa sags : unperks, overcooks Fit
2 dye me under a law which i can only subsume
means i 2 would sag : unperk, overcook Cluck & kit
Knuck & buck'd body[ody-ody-ody in death Debloom

-ery I dole A *doc's note* & it'd've been fine but 4 a dude
A mens en boothful unclockability w my 1-nite-only-*oops*
Nationstates luv men bc mens luv the maybe brood of a nuke
I hav no Canto nor Mandarin but kno what 4 who supes

up all salves of the nationstate There are rules here Shiny
International law here 4 queer bureaucratic besting
Lookit this TSA-approved-pre-text 4 smash hiney !
Happi how homeland Securitas reward the gay nesting

instinct The returning more normal : more manner'd Kept
quiet as I've been waged against ; Warned about ;   Wept

Give a white *exactly* what it is   they are
to wont   nd become a nonsensical
legislator   of reality . Here ? No $$$$$

here . Here ? Multiculturalism is hard
on reason but y a y a yu had *NOooooO*
IdE3@ ! Yr real fuccin concerned ah?,

N-Nah I mean none y'alls asses tryna write The Holy Race Secret of America !
& @ this Point in Time Count , dunno what I'd do
after all the historiographic flexin , with reason .

(& so " Where was I " (is what they wanted (to have .   Exactly .
(& so force steers flesh down before the ayes
            aye entry . Brought a plastic sampo for the glit public

& nunya asses asked eff i'd like to be liked
or looked downupon . Wooda liked the data
specific death I hear so much about but

I am just , honestly , shocked   about my being
herein the instant erection of normalcy . Like someone's baby
doll parts . An attendant of loss . Still, this Bitch

right queer , black/en disbelief : brown eyed, lookin
like my numbers , evaluated about inches & pounds.
Forced into plastic gender I am against the M/F -er like
I really am   against   the good plastic (eff there ever
was) to save my issuing ; my deployment ; my wake-up
ride (Swiveled (Still

Wet with holwater (Still in the Bar Still I like " Manager "
because wen I say " the white man did something "
all the white people do something . But , *for shame*   i thot

flinking prostrate inna wallet frot in the proviso of a second
form (& a 3rd form) of being here   I am   real
-ly being here   1nce , in the skinthicc

                          2 wice , in the far governance nd
                          3 h r i ce , my University of Iowa ID shines something
of resolution's fandom ! All barstools hold kind purpose ,

not *persons* . No explicit exhibits or expositions of readiness . For
something *else* Anything   *else* . This has all been taken or is being
saved for a non-performative friend . &   I'll leave , but before I do

(ye broke ass barlite) I will hav u kno the same fuccing way about policy,
about refusal : & about this nice White Nationalist Settler Market ya got here?
It'd b a shame if anything happened innit .

The reasonable man carries a reasonable wallet , the wallet frequently mon-
ied . The reasonable man's reasonable wallet contains a reasonable bus pass .
Now— If you are , say , staying in that body of yours , & the reasonable man
finds that body of yours an unreasonable ambulant , does he say that ...

        a) You don't look ...
        b) I'm not into ...
        c) Get those hands where I can buy 'em or I'll shoot !

Lessay somethin about property's
occupational preference : that law
luvs her thingamajigs & whosiwhatsits

&nd lessay if law total 10 / 9 of the crowd
pull purse to chest
Lessay these yt people pretty well
-adjusted 4 being pretty well off
war puppetears   Lessay *include*
a " Making of " & lessay look at me   when I'm
talkim bout chu So say the void , the self ,
the faith-money ; the ugly , impossible future
full of work & lessay you is ; always was ;
4 ever are LARPin the Late Holoscenery .

sumsumsum !LIBERTY! sumsumsum !FREEDOM!
sumsumsum!PROPERTY! sumsumsum !EFF YOU
BUY TODAY!

they'll thro ya —for free.99—
on a map .   & no ,   not ,
any old map ,   a map w street
lights & defriendsive architecture .

In the Original Liberalism   it's pronunt,,
" rights ."

Snowball Wart Money .

So thick .
Safe .

however hard cars pull   the dark tongue of tar
          it's never the ocean i hear in new york

though if i stop   hanging myself   out to dry
i see stars in Yonkers   or satellites

something glimmering   something always glimmers
my agnostic heart   still agnosticizes regretfully

still remembers the small fluorescent woodpeckers of Hawai'i
and when April cracks down on me   like an egg

slick and thick / i remember *there are only so many clouds*
somewhere it is glimmering everywhere and that sky is baldblue

surely the solution shouldn't be less anything less than

the very table setting of love , which makes possible the age

of weeping— ! what a necessary age— what a commitment

to the problem of others , of *outtheres* made *inheres* ,

which banned queers , blacks , which , is why white people ,
        as long as they stay white people ,

won't be getting any sense back . I J S ! I'm not out here like

genocide , *enslavement* , *ontological attack* . If these here are sentence

parts what I will do is HACK HACK HACK

        HA

        HA

        HE

        HE

as long as I am possible , I will not work and if I do work I will not work

for love

chained to money

chained to my refraining

fiscal potentiality .

ACKNOWLEDGEMENTS

Some of the poems in this collection borrow, quote, and transform material from Hoodie Allen's "Are U Having Any Fun," *Good Will Hunting* (1997, Gus Van Sant), The Oxford English Dictionary, Robert Alexander Anderson's "Mele Kalikimaka," *Advance of Kansas Volunteers at Caloocan* (Edison, 1899), Nicki Minaj's "Dance (Ass)," The Book of Job, Woodrow Wilson's Fourteen Points, *Into the Woods* (1986, Sondheim), "We Are Never Ever Getting Back Together," Taylor Swift, *Mean Girls* (2004, Waters), Robert Frost's "Mending Wall," Christina Sharpe's *In The Wake: On Blackness and Being*, William Faulkner's *The Sound and The Fury*, Jodi Benson's "Part of Your World," "We Didn't Start The Fire," Billy Joel, T.S. Eliot's "The Love Song of Alfred J. Prufrock," *The Notebook* (2004, Cassavetes), Frank O'Hara's "Ave Maria," Hart Crane's "Voyages," The Expendables' "Bowl for Two," Skee-Lo's "I Wish," and Naughty by Nature's "O.P.P."

"the white man asks ' is Hawai'i just lava, yet? '" is in response to the 2018 Lower Puna Eruption. "IT'S NOT A SONNET BC IT DON'T TURN" is an erasure of Woodrow Wilson's Fourteen Points.

Thanks to Magic Helicopter Press, Black Lawrence Press, and Omnidawn Books for publishing my chapbooks, where versions of these poems first appeared. Additionally, thanks to the editors and staff at *Smoking Glue Gun, Tagvverk, Nat. Brut, Pinwheel Magazine, Black Warrior Review, Vetch: A Journal of Trans* poetry and poetics, We Want It All: A Radical Anthology of Trans Poetry and Poetics, Best American Experimental Poetry 2020, Vinyl Poetry, American Chordata, The Atlas Review, American Academy of Poets' Poem-A-Day Series*, selected by Evie Shockley, *Boaat Journal, jubilat, O F Z O O S, DREGINALD, Potluck Magazine, Sixth Finch, Baest: a journal of queer affect, Bodega Magazine*, and *The Rumpus* for publishing earlier versions of these poems.

Thanks to the UCROSS Foundation, Iowa Writers' Workshop, The Cleveland State University Poetry Center, and Banff Centre for Arts and Creativity for their support.

Thank you, Lindsey Boldt, Gia Gonzales, Joyelle McSweeney, Stephen Motika, Kazim Ali, Caelan Nardone, and everyone else at Nightboat Books for making this book a reality.

Endless admiration and gratitude to the teachers, artists, and writers who continue to support my creative journey: Jayson P. Smith, Ben Krusling, Peter Meyers, Izzy Casey, Toby Altman, Stephen Ira & Liam O' Brien, Alyssa Moore, Simone White, Tracie Morris, Layli Long Solider, D.A. Powell, Tim Dyke, Joe Tsujimoto, Elizabeth Matson Foster, Carol Lee, Craig Santos Perez, Nick Mills, Tina Chang, Rachel Eliza Griffiths, Jeff McDaniel, and Gregory Pardlo.

Love you, Hilliards, always.
To Hannah Matsunaga—there is no one I'd rather be in this world with.
To Chase McCarson—I love you, futhermucker.

Rest In Peace to my first teacher, Joe Tsujimoto who once told me I might need a sentence doctor   luckily. I have avoided. treatment. I have.   survived treatment I have thought thru possibilities   available after the regime of treatment of symptoms of illness of flesh of symbolics of that ugh fuck touch need I have.   please understand if I   could be. apologetic. or just apoplectic or apocalyptic or tripping over my too big too feet on the way to the nation state's principal promise   primrose Inside language I have been at something. touching my toes.   tickiling my knowes .

everyone is happy(?????) 2o be (??????????) here (??????????????????) and the hol time I was a queer here, a queer there, and a queer that couldn't quite get quoted or appear or do better or peel into capitalist soothwall leather – like it I mean ! there isn't much good going on isn't there?

No so part anti in only toto whole analysis backward side up into the vac- uum of meaning produced by the raw material of the citizen

(I have waited until this moment (this moment of thanks) to reiterate (and also thank Ben Krusling for the form of thanks) my thankfulness for chaos and noise and resistance and possibility and brutality and rigor and forgiveness and water and orchids and brothers and bothers and the wonderful mettle making problem of   Others